The Origin of Pain and Evil

The Origin of
Pain and Evil

Robert E. Joyce

LifeCom

Published by
LifeCom
St. Cloud, Minnesota, USA

ISBN   978-0-615-25006-9

For information, address *LifeCom*, Box 1832, St. Cloud, MN 56302

Contents

Preface

The atheist could be right. No honest claim to belief in God who is infinitely good and infinitely powerful can withstand the manifest abuse and torture of children and other innocents. The God of absolute goodness and power might be a grand fantasy of escapists from reality. Unless.

Unless there is more to the story of Eden. And there must be. God is not a wimp, unable to prevent innocent persons from being bombed by the sin of their first parents. God did not simply "stand by" and let Adam and Eve transmit to their progeny a fragile and mortal human nature.

There is a reason why we were so affected by the original sin of our first parents. We must have deserved it. Infinite Love must have been "powerless" to intervene. Or else God is like a monster, allowing innocents to suffer extreme torture and death throughout history, including the holocaust and many other massacres. And then giving them an incomparable "reward" for enduring what "infinite power" could not prevent.

Is reality the *Game* of God, or are we missing an important aspect of the truth about human life here in the cosmic concentration camp?

The thoughts of this little book come from many years of prayerful reflection on our human predicament. The key idea concerning the unique origin of pain and evil came to me suddenly, in the midst of a discussion with faculty colleagues in 1964. One of them next to me gasped when he heard it. "Oh, no!" he said. But it sounded like he protested too much. Like many people, he did not want even to consider whether it was true.

My experience is that the perspective is *telling*. It begins to sketch an inner story of our origins that deepens the historical story to which we are accustomed.

More developed treatments of the ideas can be found in the books listed at the end of the present brief exposition.

The reader should feel free to contact me for further clarification, challenge, or confirmation. Some ideas might seem strange. But I think that, in the final analysis, all said here is confluent with the teachings of the Christian tradition, including the Catholic Church—to the truth of which I am totally committed for life.

Robert E. Joyce

Lifemeaning.com
robertjoyce@charter.net

Chapter One

Pain and Evil

Pain and evil are universal realities. Short of heaven itself, they can be encountered everywhere we go. How are we responding to them?

From the *Book of Job*, and through the ages of Jewish and Christian tradition, a classic view has been accepted. We are told that God "permits evil" to afflict the innocent for reasons of a greater good that we cannot possibly know in this world. This apparent scandal within our existence is said to be one of life's greatest mysteries, beyond our powers to understand. We are called to live within this 'obscurity' in fear of the Lord.

As far as it goes, such a response is good. But it begs further understanding. Genuine Faith seeks ineluctably deeper understanding. As Pope John Paul II stated in *Fides et Ratio* (1998), Faith and reason are like two wings that are critically needed for meaningful living, rising to contemplation of supreme truth.

What if there would be a more meaningful way to understand why God allows evil? What if there is a basic answer right within the mystery of why bad things happen to good people? Would we not be obliged to accept it—at least provisionally?

A Supposition

Let us put our theistic beliefs to the test. We can start by supposing that none of us—even as infants—are innocent of personal sin; that there is a personal reason *why* we inherited the sin of Adam and Eve; and that we all "die in Adam" (1 *Corinth.* 15:22) because we all sinned *with* Adam.

Why not admit the *possibility* that absolute creation—creation *ex nihilo, out of nothing*—was an *inter*-personal act of God, gifting us to *be* and inviting an immediate response? In fact, how could creation *ex nihilo*, with God alone as the agent, *not* be an infinitely free act on God's part as Giver and require an *immediately free* (finite) act on our part as receivers of the gift?

Our immediate response to the gift of *be*-ing was obviously less than fully positive. Look at us. It must have been at least partly negative. That is why we came into this world where we are totally dependent on God for redemption and are now dependent on God, as well as on our own willingness, for salvation. We are "in recovery" of being.

Dependency on God for becoming and for salvation is necessary and good. We are normally far from sufficiently dependent on God in everyday life and in the depths of our soul. But we seem totally unaware that it is our *willed* (independent) dependence on God that will make it possible for God to free us from sin, so that we can be forever independent-*with* God, self, and others. We are called to live our identity—on the cross of paradox—as beings of *both* dependence *and* independence.

Independence-*with*

We need a paradigm shift in theology and philosophy. Our primary relationship with God—quite different from our redemptive relationship—is not one of dependence, but of a certain kind of independence. We are related to God in creation *ex nihilo* by an independence-*with* God, *not* an independence-from or –of God.

We seem to be completely unaware of the originative gift of being-independent-*with* God. We are conditioned to deny *consciously* a basic truth that for a person *to be*, as such, is *necessarily* to be perfect. Perfectly independent-*with* God and all others.

Chapter Two

A Perfect Creation

If God is *infinitely* perfect, God creates only perfect beings, having perfect freedom to respond. The infinitely perfect Creator creates only perfect (finite) effects.

It is impossible for God to create *ex nihilo* anything imperfect, and so it is impossible—*out of nothing*—to create gradually through stages, as the *Book of Genesis* characterizes the beginning. Every process is necessarily imperfect, even if it is going in a positive direction. Newer stages serve to improve or diminish earlier conditions.

Whatever is imperfect is a subject undergoing a process. At every point, what is in process is imperfect and in need of development.

But God created out of nothing, not out of something perfect or imperfect. God did not create in a parceled out manner, as defective creators have to do. This perfectly creating Being must have created all persons, angelic and human together, immediately and perfectly, in an act that is not spatial or temporal at all.

And we creatures, angelic and human—as God's perfect gifts—would naturally and essentially have responded with perfect freedom. Some said, in effect, fully *yes* to the perfect (finite) goodness of their being and to the perfect (infinite) goodness of their Creator. They immediately entered everlasting glory (heaven). Others said fully *no*.

("I will not serve.") They immediately brought about thereby their own everlasting frustration of being (hell).

There were also many *human* persons who must have said *yes*-and-*no* (*maybe*) in giving their free response. Because of hesitation or a partial "no" to infinite Love, they would have immediately crashed, entering into an ontologic coma—a profound unconsciousness of *being*. They are *we*.

Even if some of us made only the slightest demurral, we failed to embrace, with our whole being, the infinite Gifter of our being as we were called to do—called by our very being to *unite fully with* God. And we went directly, if partly, against the structure of our being unique, perfect persons.

Our relatively indifferent response to the *absolutely unqualified gift* of *being* must have been the decisive cause of our largely passive-reactive kind of being that, as we awaken in the world of space and time, we find ourselves to *be*.

The *origin* of spatial and temporal existence came *through us and our maybe*. We caused the need for space and time. And here we are now, all spaced out, doing time.

God caused space and time to be, but not *ex nihilo*. *Ex aliquo* (out of something). God must have created space and time—intrinsically imperfect forms of being—out of the void and the darkness caused by our immediate response to creation *ex nihilo*.

Right from within our self-distorting selves, by our *maybe*, we caused a spiritual (ontological) Big Bang of Being—the biggest bang of all. From this explosion of our being, energy was created, from which God immediately began forming the cosmos—a prominent *part* of the process for our recovery.

Genesis, therefore, begins to tell the story of our *coming back* from the crash—of how we are be-*coming.* This cosmic coming-to-be is a significant part of our *redemptive* creation by God.

This compensational kind of creation (*ex aliquo*) is fashioned out of the devastating effects of an *originative sin, committed along with* Adam at the immediate, non-durational moment of the absolute beginning of our *be*-ing (*ex nihilo*).

Chapter Three

Originative Sin

In the beginning—the very beginning of *being* and not merely of the temporal universe—God said, "Be." The three divine Persons must have said, "Be and Be with Us in your being forever." And immediately and freely, to one degree or another, we now-fallen humans responded, "Maybe."

Our free and full response was defective to some degree and thereby created—in our own human personhood—a void in God's creation. From out of that void, God attempts to save us by the redemptive creation told in *Genesis*, through the coming of prophets, and specifically through the life, death, and resurrection of Jesus Christ.

What we have known and called creation as portrayed in *Genesis* is creation *ex aliquo*—creation out of something, namely a void, a darkness, a passivity—that *could not* have been initiated by the *infinitely* pure Act of God.

God does not create junk. Nor even junkables. But God seems to create "self-junkables." Every person, whether angelic or human, is gifted with the absolute ability for self-determination. We might call it freedom. But freedom is our ability to elicit goodness only, not evil. Our ability to will less than good is an ability that, in exercise, makes us less free.

Christian tradition teaches that perhaps a third of the angelic persons said fully *no* to God's gift and rendered themselves "junk beings." (*Revelation* 12:4,9) Perhaps also there were many, or a few, *human* persons who immediately and fully said *no* and thereby destroyed their own true freedom ever to love. Such persons would not be candidates for redemption by the Word of God any more than Lucifer and his cohorts of infamy. Their self-decimation would be complete.

We who sinned by saying *maybe*—over whom Adam was appointed head—must have *partly* trashed ourselves "on the spot." We crashed and now exist in dire need of reclamation. The *yes*—however strong or weak—in our *maybe* warrants our potential rehabilitation, even as the *no* opens us to the possibility of total self-destruction.

Understanding Why Bad Things Happen

An *originative sin* by all of us fallen creatures, personally and commonly, would seem to offer a more intelligible understanding of why "bad things happen to good people." This supposition differs appreciably from the way the origin of sin has been taken heretofore. But, in comparison, an originative sin may be much more compatible with the fear of the Lord and with the acceptance of the great mystery of the existence of evil in its broad details.

Such a way of conceiving our origins could account more fundamentally for how and why we sinned and have suffered pain. This hypothesis of *personal responsibility for originative sin* would seem to move us, more plausibly, deeper into the mystery of evil and pain and their often-devastating effects.

In a culture, such as ours, that is quite aware of the reality of *unconscious* motivation, the story of Adam and Eve could be enriched and made more understandable. In our emotional lives, *unconscious motivation caused by repression* has to have its vastly deeper counterpart *in our spiritual lives* and at the heart of our being. The spiritual is the in-depth cause of mind-body conditions. Doctrinal development on the origin of evil and suffering may be long overdue.

As it is now, we have been satisfied with saying that we cannot logically see why an infinitely perfect God would allow any suffering at all to inflict young children, the mentally incompetent, and the living saints. But suppose we recognize that every one of these earthly dwellers, along with all ordinary Joes and Janes, must have committed a pristine abuse of their own perfect, God-gifted freedom, and buried it spiritually from sight.

Suppose we all had a perfect non-temporal beginning at the moment of creation out of nothing; that we were perfect human persons with perfect freedom to determine the quality of person we would be; and that immediately we freely failed, in our first personal act of freedom, to live up to that gift of perfect being and freedom. Face to face with God—though not with divine glory—we willed, at least partly, to be given an *infinitely* perfect being, like that of the three Persons doing the giving, and not simply a *finitely perfect* one.

Our freedom-*power* was perfect. Our *act* was not. We exercised the perfect power imperfectly. *We* acted. The perfect God-gifted power did not. We acted *with and by* the perfect power. But the power does not act, nor does the act *act*. The *doer* or *agent* acts. The *person* is responsible for acting perfectly or imperfectly.

Suppose God said, "Be," but we said, "Maybe." We were freely tentative, as we might say, and that very pristine self-assumed attitude caused us to crash as candidates for beatitude, leaving us in an immense, being-constricted (ontological) coma, from which Divine Rescue was our only hope.

Suppose further that God's creation of the cosmos, reported in the *Book of Genesis*, was an ordered development of passive matter, from out of the void-in-being that was caused by our diffident response to the gift of creation. With some additional explication, we might become quite a bit more at home with the mystery of creation and sin than the traditional viewpoint seems to afford us.

We might, then, become gradually free of the blame game, wherein we blame Adam, he blames Eve, she blames the serpent, and serpent blames God. We could break the chain of blame that binds us to a false self-concept before God. We might more fully repent for being the limping kind of created persons only we could have made ourselves to be.

Chapter Four

Basic Truths

The new theistic perspective can be elucidated by articulating its basic truths. At this point, I will state a series of basic truths, including elementary comment on each of them. Some of these truths are recognizably essential to Judeo-Christian faith. Others might be understood as corollaries.

1. **God is not simply *all*-perfect (*all*-good, *all*-powerful, and the like), but infinitely so**. For Christians, God is *unlimitedly* good, powerful, loving, and so forth. God is three infinite Persons in one infinite Nature or Kind of Being.

Calling God all-good, omnipotent, and so forth is misleading. There are two radically different kinds of perfection, goodness, power, and the like: finite and infinite. God is not "all" perfect because God does not have any *finite* perfection, goodness, and power for which there could be an "all."

There is no "all" or "totality" about infinity. The idea of an "infinite totality" is contradictory. Thinking of infinity as "the whole infinity" makes God a high-class, finite being. Infinity is "beyond wholeness." Every good angel, however, can be regarded as all-good, all-powerful in his own right, albeit with goodness and power perfectly proportionate to his own *limited* being.

2. God always does perfectly, unlimitedly, and unconditionally whatever can be done. Some things are not really possible (they are contradictory, mere illusions of potency), such as God making something so heavy that even God cannot lift it, making a square circle, creating an imperfect creature, creating a perfect person without perfect freedom in that person by essence, forcing the freedom of free creatures, and so forth.

3. **God is an infinitely Loving Creator who creates by an infinitely intimate love for the creature, who is an unique person and a member of the creation community.** Even the slightest unresponsiveness to this infinitely intimate love would have caused our present plight. Failure to respond *fully* to infinite love and infinite intimacy is an "unthinkable" offense. And we surely seem not to think about it.

4. **God cannot create a being directly who is not a person-being, truly like God, able to share, perfectly and fully, if he or she wills it, the love that gifts him or her to be.** God does not create sub-personal beings *ex nihilo* directly, but only indirectly, that is, in virtue of the need that freely, if partly, rejecting created persons would have: a place or environment for trying to recover and

come back to the likeness of God in which these persons are *originatively* created.

5. God creates directly *ex nihilo* every person as a whole being with absolutely perfect freedom to respond immediately. But the cosmic creation is an indirect creation—a creation *ex aliquo* (out of something vague) as in the six days of creation and in the creation of Adam and Eve out of dust and a rib, respectively.

This cosmic creation, then, is contextual creation: done in the context of the absolute creation out of nothing wherein the whole "be-ing" of the original creatures emanates from God. Only those original created persons who said *maybe* to the gift of their being and to the goodness of their Creator enter specifically into God's cosmic creation for the sake of redemption.

Genesis, then, includes only stories of creation that are creation-for-the-sake-of-redemption—creation done out of something, not done out of nothing. The "something" would be the crashed condition of the created persons who sinned and thus became in need of restructuring (of the "reconstructive surgery" of God's redeeming Love) if they were not to fall totally away into complete self-frustration (hell).

With *unlimited* love and power, God creates perfect persons (angelic and human). God does not create directly anything that is imperfect. Imperfection comes from the defection of free-willed persons making a mess of themselves and creating a passive, insular ontological environment, such as the world we know and call the cosmos.

6. **God's created persons are (as persons) necessarily free and are perfectly free (as created directly by God).** There is no imperfection in their originative freedom as given by God. They are able to say fully *yes* to their being—or fully *no*; or, in the case of human persons, *maybe* (*yes* and *no*).

Their originative act—their first act of *be*-ing—was free of temptation. They were perfect and untemptable. (Only imperfect beings need testing to see whether their freedom is intact.) Theirs was a *purely* active potency, the sheer ability to *do without being-done-to*.

7. **All persons—angelic and human—are created perfectly free; they inevitably determine themselves to be forever related *with* God or *without* (against) God.**

Each one determines personal destiny forever. No one else, including God, could possibly be *decisive* in the ultimate decision of the freely gifted person.

8. **Angelic persons, in primal simplicity of likeness to God, had no way of saying *maybe*, because they do not have the *kind* of receptivity that humans have.** Theirs was a superior kind of being. But human persons were created "a little less than the angels" (*Psalms* 8:6) and have a double receptivity. A receptivity of their essence for their being and a receptivity within their essence of matter for form. The first kind of receptivity is that of willing to be or not to be (a receptivity quite like the angels). The second kind admits of the receptivity of being

able to will to be in degrees—to be only so much the way God gifted them to be in essence.

God creates perfect creatures perfectly. God cannot create *out of nothing*, simply, an imperfect creation of any kind. If imperfection occurs in anyone, it must be *totally* the fault of *that* created *person*. Such a person is perfectly *free to affirm*, and yet also *able to deny*, the goodness of being and of God. Perfect (finite) freedom, as the gift of God, has about it no imperfection at all.

Divine freedom, by contrast, includes a freedom to create or not to create—out of nothing—whomever God wills to be. There is no Divine ability, however, to be either good or evil (to sin), as there is inherently for created persons. God's freedom is of a different kind: infinite.

Finite persons are not able to *create* out of nothing, but they are *able to will* to be "nothing"—which choice only makes them *distortedly* the something they are, but cannot make them into the nothing they really can will or attempt to be. Annihilation, however, is not a real "option."

9. **God creates *directly* persons *only*; sub-humans and inanimate matter must have been created by God *indirectly*.** We know this because sub-personal creatures are not capable of being, in themselves, perfect. They are unable to receive (or reject) themselves. They lack intellect and will.

Sub-personal creatures (from molecules to monkeys) must be the result of a fallen world or of the *needs* of a fallen world. Even in the Garden of Eden, the animals and

17

plants that are said to be there reflect, at least, a Fall-to-be. (And, in the new supposition, they bespeak a Fall that already had occurred: *originative* sin).

Matter itself is *not imperfect*; but the *passive* kind of matter, of which space and time are inherent dimensions, *is* imperfect. *Self-passivized* matter resulted from the abysmal failure of our transparently receptive being. Our purely active receptivity was made, by our originative sin, to be "sluggishly receptive," to say the least.

10. Along with angels, humans are created with the personhood-capacity to respond to their creation out of nothing immediately and unconditionally with a *yes*.

If humans *de facto* respond with less than a full *yes*— even if only slightly—they are thoroughly in need of redemption. They damage themselves shamefully before God. If they respond with a complete *no*, they are instantly lost. If they respond with a full *yes* they confirm themselves in everlasting beatitude with God and with all other totally affirming creatures—angelic and human.

As created immediately by God, human beings are fully persons and fully free to determine the *kind* of persons they will be—good persons or bad. Saying that humans are fully persons means that they are persons by nature or essence.

Human persons are not such that they merely *can come* to full humanity. Those who think that humans are now, as we find ourselves, simply potentially full persons confuse functional potency with natural potency. The distinction is crucial and is addressed in Chapter Six.

Basic Truths

What we know as matter or the material dimension (energy, corporeality, and such) of humans in the cosmos is quite paradoxical. This passive matter is *both* negative and positive. It is the gravely distorted result of human persons misusing immediately the perfect potency to be willing-to-*be*. But it is also the awesome means for God to create them *ex aliquo*—to bring them back out of the void in freedom and being that they had created in themselves.

If the human persons we know in this world had said a full-hearted *yes*—and not a partial-hearted yes—to their creation out of nothing, they would not be here. But they would still have matter—perfect matter or *untrammeled receptivity*—and would be fulfilled in heaven by their act of fully receiving being—by their own act of *self-determination to receive fully* their being.

Human *ability* (capacity) to be willing only *to be in degrees*, as well as (eventually) to be willing or unwilling totally, means that human persons have redeem-*ability* built right into their essence. In the case that they sin, originatively and untemptedly, by giving a less than full *yes* and not a total *no*, the Word of God, Christ Jesus, works with their measure of *yes* to redeem and save them.

These ten basic perspectives help to form the basis for an assurance about the new theistic claims. Our participation in the Faith, especially relating to creation and sin, is destined to deepen by virtue of knowing and living these truths.

Chapter Five

Originative Creation

How could the originative creation of perfect persons with perfect freedom have "occurred"? How did it "happen"? How could it *be*?

A specifically Christian account of creation would involve the Trinity of infinite and eternal Persons. These Persons are the Agents of originative creation and are united with One Another in glory.

These Divine Persons create, *out of nothing and in absolute freedom*. They do not "need to" create at all, but do so out of infinitely free generosity. At a durationless "point" within eternity, God *loves into being* mega-multitudes of persons, angelic and human. We keep wanting to "put a point" on it or to it. But God's acts are "pointless."

This creation *ex nihilo* is an act of infinite Being. The created persons are perfect and immediately able to create their own destiny in accord—or in discord—with their uniquely gifted nature. As creatures, however, they are *not* able to create *anything* out of nothing—much less themselves. They are definitively receptive (finite) beings.

Each created person is perfect: perfectly free, and perfectly himself or herself with the ability to receive fully. The question of "equality" is not directly relevant, since this creational moment of being is perfect for each, even though everyone is unique and thus different from all others. And we know from Christian revelation that there are choirs and a hierarchy among angels.

Only persons are complete beings, emanating directly from the heart of God. Sub-personal creatures cannot come into being that way. They are intrinsically imperfect, self-unreceptive beings that *both* symptomatize the originative fragmentation done by self-afflicting human persons *and* serve the sacramentive promise of salvation for those humans who repent.

The originative creation brought into being different kinds of person and their different ontological degrees of personhood (e.g., there are levels of angelic hosts). But the "lower degree" of personhood of some is not because they lack anything due to them. Everything they are is fully proportionate to the degree that they reflect directly and intrinsically the Divine Trinity of Persons.

This gifted difference is thus not like the hierarchy in the cosmos, where it can be reasonably said that plants are not only lower forms of life than animals, but that they are more *lacking in* perfection than animals are: i.e., plants are less like persons than are animals. Molecules of inorganic substance are among the lowest forms of passively material being and are least like human persons, but still have some likeness of feature. Like persons, they too are unique beings and are related to all other beings in the universe, even if incompletely.

At the moment of creation (*ex nihilo*), the absolutely receiving created person is entirely free to receive well and fully his or her being and to receive the being of the

Creator—differently, yet proportionately. At that instant, total and immediate intimacy and ecstatic union with God forever is an absolute potentiality—an active, not a passive, potency. At this primal moment, the created person is naturally, functionally, and totally free to say *yes* to God's gift: his or her being.

By contrast, our present, even best conditions for freedom in the cosmic world are conditions of a natural and functional freedom that are seriously damaged. We are dysfunctionally free as far as we ourselves being able to recover our perfection of freedom that was gifted to us at the moment of creation.

How then can the created person, in the fallen condition, freely choose to be with God? How can you and I will or intend *fully* to *be-with* the gift of being-at-all and of being self that we are naturally gifted to be? How can we *be-with* and *be-within* our own *being* perfectly?

Face to Face in Act, but Not in Glory

Perhaps, we can begin to gain a shaft of light on how to recover and *be*-with God by reviewing how we got into the "human predicament." How could any created person be perfect and perfectly free but, in the same moment, abuse the *act* of freedom?

First, we have to realize firmly that this "moment" of creation *ex nihilo* is *not* a moment of *time* or of any other kind of duration. There is no lag. Everything happens at once, 'as it is in heaven.' There is no prior presentation of alternatives to the will that the agent can consider deliberatively, even quickly, before making a decision.

The Origin of Pain and Evil

In response to the act of originative creation, the *decision* whether to affirm God's gift that is being received by us is *created*, not "made." The created person creates, out of the limits—not defects—of his or her own perfect being, who he or she *wills* to be.

God and the creature are "face to face" at that mutually creative moment of origin within eternity. But the creature does not gaze on the *glory* of God, as would be or will be the case once, or if, the creature *affirms fully* the goodness of the being of the gift and of the Giver.

Thomas Aquinas has indicated that we *could* not say *no* to God once we enter eternal glory. This is true. But it is not because we would be overwhelmed by divine Glory. Infinite Love never overwhelms the beloved. (Only sinful beings can be overwhelmed by infinite glory. But that is because of their defectiveness, not because of God's infinite goodness and power.)

Purely active receivers of being receive without being "done to"—without any passivity at all about them. They are giftedly pure finite acts of being and doing. They are active potencies to *be-with* God, self, and all others.

In heaven, we "could not" say *no*, because we *would* not say *no*, having given our pristine, full, and consummated *yes* to the gift of being and of *being with* God. Our responsive *yes* would be gifted to God from the core of our being.

Perfect bliss, then, would not be God's doing alone, if we are really free persons. God could not *force* us to say *yes* freely. Final union is that of an infinite act of necessarily free love with a finite act of necessarily free love.

Chapter Six

The Creation Decision
and the Consequences

The moment of creation *ex nihilo*, then, can be generally acknowledged. Certain main factors or dimensions can be considered as ontologically immediate or "simultaneous." One might refer to the ABC's of the originative moment of creation.

Dimension A: God's Gifting Act. The infinite act of God's free and full *gifting* of being, including the gifting to us of the *opportunity to receive* our own being with our whole heart freely and fully—or to refuse to receive, wholly or partially.

Dimension B: The Created Person's Receiving Act. The created person's gifted being as being *received by that person*, and that same person as being challenged—by his or her very gifted being—to say fully *yes* to the gift and the Giver.

Dimension C: The Created Person's Responding Act. The actual act of the created person—the free response to *be-ing*—that determines his or her destiny. This supreme, immediate, signature act of the created person is necessarily either fully *yes*, fully *no*, or *yes-no* (*maybe*).

A full *yes* to this gift of being-at-all and to the gift of being-this-person would co-determine (with God) the person's ecstatic union with God and with all other fully affirming creatures forever in perfect (creaturely) likeness to the Triune God. A full *no* to this gift of being-at-all and of being-this-person would exclusivistically self-determine the person's being as totally opposed to being-at-all and to being-in-relation-with God.

Even hell-choosers, however, *cannot not be* and *cannot not be related* to God and to all other beings, despite their whole-hearted desire not to *be*. This condition of full opposition creates hell, where they "get their way" in all their individualistic impotence.

A partial *yes* and partial *no* (a *maybe*) to this gift of being and of being-who one is—along with similar responses from other *maybe*-sayers of *varying degrees* of *yes*—determines the respondents into the condition of a grave distortion of being. They thus absolutely need redemption by God from this definite distrust of the being God gave them to be.

The Unique Act of Freedom

Why would any creatures not choose God fully at the moment of creation? How could they be perfect and not choose perfectly the perfect way to go?

This first act of *freedom* of the created person is not really a choice as choices occur in space and time, wherein the effects of self-damaged freedom are functionally everywhere in evidence. Our limping functional freedom in this life (after the fact of the fall) cannot be used mainly as a base for our understanding of God's originative gift of pristine natural ("supernatural," God-intended) and functional freedom. (At the point of creation we had *perfect* freedom—both natural and functional freedom.) There are no prior "options" passively presented to a passively receiving mind and heart, as is the case in our present milieu.

Rather, this first, signature act of freedom is like no other (subsequent) act of freedom *could* be. This act of prime freedom *creates* (out of oneself) the course of activity or action. It is not like choosing to go down one road as opposed to alternative routes. In such a case, the roads or options are there ahead of the choice. But this first act of *freedom* "creates its own road, while traveling it."

Freedom in Space and Time

Even now in space and time our morally significant acts of choice are not specifically a choosing of already laid courses of action. They might be considered that way only secondarily. Primarily, our free acts are acts of self-determination whereby we literally, in the very act of choice itself, determine what *kind* of human person we are going to *be*—whether we get a chance to fulfill it in a course of action or not.

Choosing to help or to refuse to help a needy passing stranger is morally significant *not mainly* because a fellow human being will either receive or lose out on something most needed. Our gift of help or its deprivation will happen by our own volition—for better or for worse. By a good-willing choice, we create within ourselves a bit larger, richer kind of being or personhood. By a bad-willing choice, we cause within ourselves a bit smaller, poorer kind of being or personhood.

The Origin of Pain and Evil

Every moral choice made by a human person (even one who is in the world of space and time) is critical. Personhood itself—applicable to all persons—is either honored or dishonored. Even when we do not get the opportunity to carry out our chosen action to help someone—if he or she is, say, saved by a surprise beneficial happening before we can get the helpful supplies we deliberately intend to obtain—our choice itself or willingness (not mere wishing or wanting) determines and tells us and all others just what kind of human person we are or are becoming.

If we had chosen to refuse help to the stranger, but the same fortuitous kind of help came to him or her from someone else, we can realize that our refusal was a *choice that did us in*, not the stranger; and we have lessened our participation in our own humanity and in that of all others just by *being unwilling* to be a person-helper.

All of our exercise of human personhood is demeaned by our goodness-denying choices (however good the consequences might seem to be). "Judicious theft" of Company records might seem to yield good consequences for many people, but is unjust in itself.

Our human personhood, moreover, is enhanced by our goodness-affirming choices (however bad the effects might seem to be). Refusing to abort our child might seem to result in bad consequences of severe inconvenience for child and parents. But it is good and just in itself.

The Difference between Natural and Functional Freedom

In this world, we must recognize the difference between natural and functional freedom. If a being is a human person, natural freedom is one of the prime, necessary attributes. Just by being a *person,* the being is naturally able to choose the *quality* of person he or she will be. As an embryo, infant, or senile member of the human community, the particular person may not have developed or may have lost the *functional* freedom to intend something, but this member is *naturally* free, no matter how impaired. Even if the nature is fully twisted, as in hell, each person as a person is essentially and naturally free.

The distinction between natural and functional applies to all living beings and to all natural substances. An embryo rabbit has the *natural* capacity to hop, even though it does not have the *functional* ability—yet. Even an inorganic molecule can be said to have natural properties, so there can still be conditions under which those properties will not function or wherein the functions will be impaired or diminished.

Among purely spiritual beings, wherein freedom is specifically involved, we might say that the good angels exercised their natural and functional freedom perfectly from the word "go"—or rather from God's word, "Be"! At the moment of creation, they had perfect natural and functional freedom and exercised it perfectly. The bad angels exercised their perfect natural and perfect functional freedom perversely, creating a total personal block between natural and functional freedom.

By saying, in effect, "I will not serve," the angelic person totally perverted his functional freedom to say anything else forever. He destroyed his own functional freedom; but he did not destroy who or what he is, including his being a naturally free creature. His natural freedom remains, but is totally impotent because of what he did to it functionally. He fully *willed* self-destruction of his genuine freedom about *be*-ing.

In the context of this perspective on freedom, we can begin to assess how and why we are in the "human predicament." We are perfect created persons of both spirit and matter who could have said fully *yes*. Our spirit and matter were created perfect and as totally active—both the spiritual and the material dimensions of our being were totally active and *not at all passive. There was no passivity to our being as issued from the infinitely loving Power of God.*

We ourselves created all the passivity that we now find in our souls and bodies, our spirit and matter, our minds and hearts. We are overwhelmed in passivity and impotent to do anything fully effective to eradicate this condition. We can only make *movements of good will in that direction.* God's saving activity does "the rest."

We are vastly dysfunctional in freedom and love, but not totally so, as are our fellow created persons who said simply *no*.

We are laced with dysfunctional freedom while retaining necessarily the natural freedom that we *are*. We did not totally *block ourselves from ourselves* and from God by our own abuse of our perfect natural and perfect functional freedom at the moment of receiving creation.

The Creation Decision

But it is folly to think that our "first freedom" is the same kind of freedom that we have now—after the great act of self-abasement has occurred. So, as we awaken to our human plight in the cosmos, we must do all we can to understand what freedom is and can be, independent of our rather dysfunctional exercise of it. Only through the best of that weakened kind of understanding can we begin to appreciate who we are and why bad things "happen" to us.

All our pain and evil are coming from multitudes of sources, but ultimately from our personal selves and through the initial abuse of our perfect, God-gifted freedom.

Chapter Seven

The Challenge

We can hardly deny *originative* sin, if we can accept as true the ten basic propositions noted in Chapter Four.

Actually, those who would balk at the reality of a personal originative sin have the main burden of proof. Between the perfect creation done by God directly *out of nothing* and the grossly imperfect, if good-true-beautiful, world of space and time there lies the missing link: our *originative* sin. Adam and Eve's original sin in Eden could only be derivative of *that* sin and a "wake up call" on how weak they already were, abandoning God with hardly a hassle.

God does not create impaired being. We do. Above all, we do it personally. While there are many real causes of our suffering other than we ourselves, we are still the *ultimate* cause of any evil or pain that we might ever have to suffer. Without our first personal sin, none of the conditions of this world's pain and ugliness would be for us. Only our Redeemer (or any redemptive partner) suffers *ultimately* unjustly in this world. Jesus is our personal Savior much more intimately than we may have imagined.

But we resist admitting the deeply intimate character of the sin from which Jesus saves us. We have repressed our originative gift of perfect freedom and our immediate, imperfect exercise of it. Now, in the insularity of our existence, we are unconsciously (repressively) denying the fact of the act.

This denial is itself a spiritual act that needs to be raised to consciousness. Theologians and philosophers are ever to be challenged to help people become aware of the "inside story" of our creation and redemption. They need not rely exclusively on the hitherto largely "outside stories" we have been used to hearing and reciting.

We need to exercise the two wings of faith and reason in order to rise toward truth, as Pope John Paul II encouraged believers to do. (*Fides et Ratio*, 1998) Both passivistic servility to common ways of conceiving and aggressivistic flights into Gnostic exclusionism must be avoided. The basic principles within faith and reason ever reinforce and ramify one another.

A Copernican Revolution in theology is long overdue. If we were to make such a breakthrough or turnaround, we would see that we are not only inheritors of the sin of Adam and Eve at the beginning of history and of our *becoming* (our coming back to being). We are the *cause*, from the beginning of our *be-ing*, as to why we even began to exist in the community of Adam and Eve and did not enter freely and immediately into the glory of God.

Despite our speaking of the sunrise and sunset even today, we know that the sun has never "risen" in the geophysical history of the universe. Rather, the earth keeps turning. Similarly, the *origin* of our sin and of all the pain and evil that it spawns is not only Adam's "history-making" sin, but also *our own originative sin* that caused us to crash and to be included in the "fallen community" of Adam and Eve. Even now we continue to exercise imperfectly our freedom to be who we will to be.

Our "sunrise thinking" about the origin of human pain and evil needs to stop. We fully deserved the inheritance. Consciousness-raising of a spiritual and ontological kind needs to come forward. Consigning the origin of evil and of the suffering of "innocents" to the 'obscurity of God' is escapist; it yields yet another symptom of our unconscious *unwillingness* to know "the answer" to the fiercest question in theology: why apparently innocent people have to suffer.

By supposing that we were created perfect, out of absolutely nothing, and that we immediately responded, out of perfect freedom, by not saying *fully yes,* we know *why* "bad things happen to good people" and a whole lot more. We have only to *admit the truth repentantly* in order to be much more at home with the mystery of evil and of pain. Much more grateful for the hope of final rescue. And much more able *sincerely to receive* God's unlimited mercy and infinitely loving salvation.

Robert E. Joyce, Ph.D., is *professor emeritus* at
St. John's University, Collegeville, Minnesota

Afterword

Affirming Created Persons in Freedom

The Origin of Pain and Evil underscores the urgency of a simple truth of human life. Every child needs *affirming love* in order to flourish as a human being. The smile of a radiant mother cuddling her baby in her arms can be the single most wholesome experience for that little person's life. The baby feels warmly welcome and strengthened in his or her unique being, not simply valued or treasured.

The mother's smiling care and affirming love reaches into the child's unconscious life where the truth of creation reveals the greatest affirmation of all: God's affirming *gift* of being.

The gift, however, was not completely received. So, God established a family for the fallen person. Parents provide love and nurture to each child, a dependent person, newly-initiated in space and time. By their affirming love for the child, the parents participate specially in the redemptive creation.

By gradually learning to receive this love well, the child participates in a critical reparation. Within the mind and heart of the little one, there is, also unconsciously, the healing touch of God. Redeeming love runs as deep as creating love, and is offered to the child unconditionally.

This eternal love re-calls the little person into the *community of being*, through the love of mother and father, family and friends. All ensuing growth-and-development in this world is rich with increasing opportunities. The growing person is invited once again to receive the gift of pristine creation (out of nothing) by participating willingly in the redemptive creation through which this person was conceived and born.

Many infants and growing children, however, are not genuinely affirmed by their mothers and fathers. They might live their whole lives deprived of being affirmed. Other unaffirmed youngsters come to an affirmation experience, somewhere along the line. Even if only in adulthood, some persons happen to encounter someone who is meaningful in their lives and who delights in their being. As psychiatrist Conrad Baars delineates in his book, *Born Only Once*: *The Miracle of Affirmation* (Quincy, Ill.: Franciscan Press, 2001), human beings need an emotional birth that is beyond the physical. They cannot give this psychic birth to themselves. They must await the gift from someone else, and be ready to receive it.

Beyond emotional birth, the Christian faith teaches the need for everyone to be "born again" spiritually. By the affirming action of Baptism, God loves us as unique persons. We can accompany this affirmation of our being by shouts of joy and by feelings of spiritual exhilaration, or simply by a quiet receiving. This "third birth" yields the functional potential for everlasting union with God.

So, the conversion of our being calls for three births. Our mother's giving us physical birth is a major move toward our becoming able to say *yes* to life and love. Then, her smile and care may or may not be sufficiently loving. But someone needs to love us well enough emotionally and holistically to give us the second birth, to lift us into the level where a flourishing personality can develop.

Afterword

Besides these two natural births, and compensating for their defects, we need the supernatural birth of Divine grace enlivening our souls and bodies. God alone can give us this spiritual birth, generally through the sacred ministry of the organization of believers established for that purpose.

If sufficient development does not happen in the course of our brief, temporal life, this process will have to occur, as it were, abruptly upon our death—whether this mortal passing takes place in the mother's womb or after a long life. A sudden and unprovided death is a tragedy, not because Infinite Love is at fault, but because our *maybe* condition needs all the *yes*-development it can attain. We need this be-coming to increase our recovery that ministers to a final act of repentance at the moment of death. At that moment, on its non-temporal side, when we are again emphatically in the Presence of God, we will either rise beyond or fall back into our passivity. We will either exercise adequately or abandon completely our purely active ability to love God, ourselves, and all others.

The mainly inside story of creation is the story of our freedom, its nature, and its consequences. *The Origin of Pain and Evil* calls for a deeper reading of the *Genesis* story of creation—between the lines and within its aura. The challenge is to get in touch with our being and the truth of our freedom. We can realize gratefully that we are eternally affirmed, both in being created and in being rescued from our first response. Finally, the largely untold story of our *freedom* profoundly encourages our *yes* to God and to the entire *community of being.*

Reading Available from *LifeCom* in the **Two Creations Series**

Affirming Our Freedom in God:
The Untold Story of Creation
(LifeCom, 2001) 100 pages.

The Cry of Why beneath the Holocaust; Are We Hiding Something? God Freely Creates Our Freedom to Create, *et al*.

Facing the Dark Side of Genesis:
A New Understanding of Ourselves
(LifeCom, 2008) 84 pages.

The Genesis Gap; Originative Sin; Theology of the Person's Being; Two Creations: Originative and Redemptive; Consequences for a Life of Faith, *et al*.

A Perfect Creation:
The Light behind the Dark Side of Genesis
(LifeCom, 2008) 170 pages.

From Chaos to Cosmos; The Missing Infinity of God; God's Intimate Act of Creation; The Meaning of Evil and Its Cause, *et al*.

The following comprehensive volume may be pre-ordered:

When God Said Be, We Said Maybe:
An Inside Story of the Creation, the Crash, and the Recovery
(LifeCom, 2009) 480 pages

Booklets:

The Origin of Pain and Evil
(LifeCom, 2008) 40 pages

The Immaculate Conception: An Inside Story
(LifeCom, 2008) 20 pages

LifeCom
Box 1832, St. Cloud, MN 56302
Lifemeaning.com

www.ingramcontent.com/pod-product-compliance
Lightning Source LLC
Chambersburg PA
CBHW031335040426
42443CB00005B/352